Waynesburg College Library
Waynesburg, Pa. 15370

D1592277

Northampton Massachusetts
Architecture & Buildings

BY THE SAME AUTHOR:

Early Christian and Byzantine Architecture (1962)

The Architecture of the Roman Empire:
   I *An Introductory Study* (1965)
   II *Cities and Towns* (forthcoming)

The Pantheon—Design, Meaning, and Progeny (1975)

Northampton Massachusetts
Architecture & Buildings

William L. MacDonald

Northampton Bicentennial Committee 1975

to the memory of Charles H. Lufkin 1918-1961

Copyright © 1975 by the City of Northampton, Massachusetts
All rights reserved.

Library of Congress Catalog Card Number 75-4239
ISBN 0–9600828–1–6
Printed in the United States of America

Library of Congress Cataloging in Publication Data
MacDonald, William Lloyd.
    Northampton Massachusetts: Architecture & Buildings
    Bibliography: p.
    Includes Index.
    1. Architecture—Northampton, Mass.
NA735.N68M33   720'.9744'23   75–4239
ISBN 0–9600828–1–6

*This book was set in Palatino type by Dix Typesetting Company
Inc., Syracuse, New York. It was printed by The Meriden
Gravure Company, Meriden, Connecticut on Mohawk's Navajo
Warm White Text, and bound by Haddon Bindery, Inc., of
Camden, New Jersey.*

Acknowledgements

I have had help from a number of people, especially from the members of the Publication Sub-Committee of the City of Northampton Bicentennial Committee, who have supported the project from the beginning: Richard Hendel (who designed the book), David B. Neal (who made the map), Tom C. Redinger, Ann Reinke (in charge of promotion and sales), Ann R. Roche (Vice Chairman, who typed the manuscript), Roger E. Roche (who saw the book through the press), John F. Skibiski, Jr. (Chairman), Jean-Ann Spencer, Wilfred D. Spencer, Jr. (who contributed most of the first four sections of the Reading List), Ellen J. Wampler, and David A. Wampler.

Part of the factual data was compiled, and my photographs printed, by Janet C. Smith, and I am indebted to her for her careful work. I would also like to thank Helen E. Searing, who read the manuscript critically, and Barbara E. Satz, who did the same and who generously helped with the photography. All of the photographs were taken in the Fall and Winter of 1974 except numbers 1, 15, 29, 79, 86, and 112, which were provided by the Smith College Slide and Photograph Collection, and number 72, courteously supplied by Professor B. M. Shaub.

These pages are inscribed to the memory of an old and close friend who loved the United States and its wonderful buildings.

William L. MacDonald

NOTE TO THE READER

The numbers in the margins refer to the illustrations. At the end of the book there is a map, keyed to the illustration numbers; a list of books about Northampton, its buildings, and related matters; and an index. When the names of architects or architectural firms are known they are given with the illustrations of their buildings. Some of the dates are only approximations.

110741

1. View of central Northampton about 1878, from the top of College Hall tower, Smith College, looking east

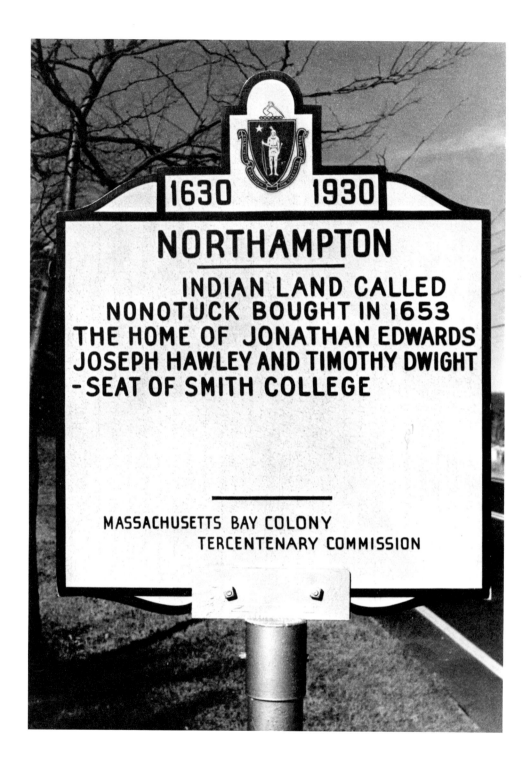

ARCHITECTURE and buildings form a surprisingly accurate—and readable—record of taste. Nearly every American style and building fad from early times right up to today is mirrored along Northampton's streets. This book takes a close, affectionate look at this gallery of buildings, good and not so good alike, and uses them to make a modest excursion into the nature and meaning of American architecture. By examining the variety of designs in Northampton buildings, by asking where this variety comes from and what it means in American culture, much can be discovered that applies to other cities and towns. Northampton is in many ways a traditional, typical city whose architectural heritage has been fairly well preserved, while at the same time it has the usual complement of modern structures, some of good quality. Thus it presents on a comprehensible scale that ever so American mixture of old and new, good and bad, and garish and restrained that makes the American architectural scene so exhilarating and mystifying. This book, then, represents an attempt to evoke something of the appearance of Northampton in the mid-seventies as the Bicentennial of the nation approaches, and makes some suggestions about why our surroundings look the way they do.

*   *   *   *   *

ON a late winter afternoon about 1878 or so, an unknown photographer carried his bulky plate camera up to the top of the tower of College Hall, then newly built. Facing west toward the Connecticut River he took an exposure of the central part of the town below him. The result shows what the area from the corner of Main and State Streets to the fall of ground beyond the First Church looked like then. Right below him was the foot of Elm Street. There to the left was the Mansion House, an inn, standing where St. Mary's Church is now. To the right the shadow of the old Baptist Church tower falls across the picture. The most conspicuous building is the Victorian Edwards Church with its spire, which had been completed a few years before. Beyond, such landmarks as City Hall and the First Church stand out. In the middle ground the Fire Station, then called the Engine House, can be seen with its original tower, later lopped off and replaced by one at the near side of the building. At the far left is a plain, New England-style white wooden church where the Elks' building now stands on Center Street. And far to the right the front part of Memorial Hall dimly appears, while in the middle foreground a freight house, originally built for the New Haven-Northampton canal (long

SITE OF THE FREIGHT HOUSE
1835 — 1847
NORTHAMPTON — NEW HAVEN CANAL
THIS CANAL PASSED UNDER
MAIN STREET THROUGH A STONE
ARCHWAY, THENCE UP STATE STREET
ENDING AT THE "HONEY POT" ON THE
CONNECTICUT RIVER.
THE NORTHAMPTON HISTORICAL SOCIETY, 1941

5. The north side of the westernmost portion of Main Street

defunct by the time the photograph was taken) stands at the corner of Elm and State Streets. The Hampshire County Court House was not yet built, and Main Street was unpaved. The effect of the time exposure was to erase all motion, but a horse stood patiently near the fire house, and a drayman with a load of casks rested his team on Elm Street near the Mansion House.

A picture taken from exactly the same spot nearly a century later
2 shows how this part of town has changed. The Mansion House, the freight house, the former Edwards Church, and other buildings have
4 disappeared. But the Fire Station, First Church, and City Hall still stand, while many new structures, unknown to the photographer of 1878, have been added. Fire, demolition, and decay have taken their toll, their effects balanced by enterprise and a natural urge to change and renovate. Some buildings and areas of the town remain as they were, while others have been changed utterly, sometimes more than once.

The preservation of part of a town while other parts are caught up in a process of radical change affects even individual buildings, as in the case of older downtown buildings whose ground floor store-fronts have been face-lifted. At the same time these processes give a town its architectural character—its mix, so to speak, of old and new, and the fashions and fads of different decades and indeed of different
5, 145 centuries not infrequently stand side by side. It is this quality, result-ing from an almost random preservation of buildings of various periods, that accounts for much of the interest and charm of a city such as Northampton. But to discuss these buildings in a row along a street, one after another, would often mean that jarring changes in time and style would have to be made repeatedly, so in the pages that follow the buildings and architecture of Northampton are dealt with according to their style and period. With some exceptions they lie within ready walking distance of the center of the town; the excep-tions lie in Leeds, in Florence, and out by the town borders. Not all of the significant buildings in Northampton could be included; the discussion is selective. And the divisions that follow are broad and general, causing now and again some blurring of stylistic niceties and continuities.

Colonial & Georgian Buildings

It used to be thought that early settlers often built simple log cabins, the kind made of trimmed but unsawn round logs laid up on a simple rectangular plan, notched and protruding at the corners. But it now appears that this was a myth given currency by supporters of William Henry Harrison, such as Daniel Webster, in the presidential campaign of 1840 when log cabins were invoked as symbols of homely integrity. But few if any of them existed in early New England, for the colonists built hand-framed houses and churches almost exclusively. That is, they constructed massive supporting frames of hardwood, the various beams and braces of which were grooved and pegged together like some huge piece of cabinet work, which was then covered over with boards on the outside and laths and plaster on the inside. This is a very different kind of building from a log cabin, which has no frame and where the walls are the supporting structure. But the colonists   6
did make plain, usually small, buildings of stout timbers roughly squared from logs with a saw or an axe. The corners of these were   7
secured by cutting back and lapping the timbers, and the chinks were filled with splinters and moss.

Most early buildings, then, were framed of wood, continuing one or another preference brought over directly from England. The most popular mode for dwellings was "five over five," a house-front with   8
a central entranceway flanked by pairs of windows, with five second-story windows positioned directly above, as simple in its concept as contemporary grave stones. The salt box form, with its back roof   9
sloping out in a lean-to form over the second story for extra space,   10
was often built. Most such early houses had fairly small windows. It should be borne in mind that a number of our examples have of necessity been repaired and restored, and sometimes they have been altered, as when porches have been added and details of windows and dormers changed over long periods of time. A considerable ele-   11
gance could be achieved with the five-over-five, especially when the   12
details were carried out by artist-craftsmen. No wonder the basic concept reappeared in strength in the twentieth century, not just because people were nostalgic for the past, or romanticized it, but also because such houses are both practical and handsome.

Waynesburg College Library
Waynesburg, Pa.   15370

Once in a while one will be seen with seven openings over seven, or three over three. These latter are usually of quite early date. Sometimes, whatever the window arrangement, the second story will overhang the first somewhat. When this happens the building is known as a garrison house, a type derived from the earliest fortified colonial houses of the seventeenth century. As time passed the overhang became a mere reminiscence—though it did give somewhat more space in the second story for a given size of foundation—and increased emphasis was given the entranceway, in order to be in tune with other, contemporary, houses. Northampton has a number of well-preserved examples of these rather aristocratic white-painted dwellings. Their proportions vary somewhat and the dates are sometimes matters of discussion, but that these houses record faithfully a way of life and an attitude toward building design is not in doubt.

Two or three rows of them have been preserved, and it takes little effort to see them much as they were seen so long ago. One has to subtract from one's vision pavements, poles, wires, and signs, and sometimes added ells and garages. But the rest is the same: the houses proper, the distances between them, their color (white exterior paint came into common use in the early 1700's), the trees, and the climate. A good place to try to evoke the original effect is along South

7. Detail of 6

8. The Parsons House, 58 Bridge Street, traditionally dated 1658

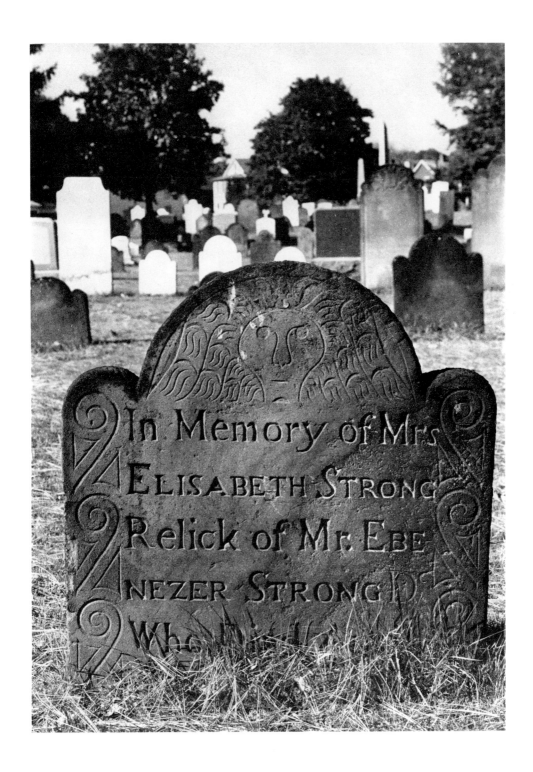

10. The Griffin House, 262 Bridge Street, 1700
11. The Hankins House, 197 Elm Street, 1730

14. *Doorway of 13*

15. *The Damon House, 46 Bridge Street, 1812; Isaac Damon was an architect and builder. The roof balustrade and the picket fence are gone*
16. *134–148 South Street*

17. *The Drury House, 134 South Street, about 1713*
18. *The Clapp House, 148 South Street, 1760*

19. The Strong House, 144 South Street, 1800

16 Street, where three houses whose dates span most of the 1700's stand
17 in line. The forms of the oldest house suggest its early date, for it has
    smallish windows and, in contrast to the others, a fairly modest
18 though nicely worked entranceway. In the next, built a couple of
    generations later, the windows have become taller. The entranceway
    is more elaborate in that its classical elements, derived ultimately
    from the architecture of ancient Greece and Rome, project further
19 out from the body of the house. The youngest of the three, built at
    the turn of the century, has the most window space in comparison to
    the whole front surface of the house. Though the porch may be later
    than the house proper it does show the tendency, which developed
    strongly in the coming decades, to shelter the entranceway with a
165 porch or a broad "piazza." Later, no American house could be with-
    out one. The need for a compact, defensible house had by then long
    since ceased and fashions had changed.

    Throughout the 1700's there was another powerful influence that
    worked to shape American houses, and that was English Georgian
    architecture, seen in its more majestic colonial form, for example, at
    restored Colonial Williamsburg in Virginia. There, as in England,
    brick predominated. But in Northampton almost every house was of
    wood; the age of brick was yet to come (commercial buildings will be
    discussed later on). The influence of the Georgian style was neverthe-
    less immense. The symmetry inherent in pairs of facade windows
    centered round the door, for example, is Georgian, and so are the
    classically-inspired entranceways. Doors flanked by fluted pilasters
18 and capped by triangular pediments recalling ancient Mediterranean
    temple fronts were hallmarks of English Georgian design. Above all,
    the sense of balance and repose in these houses, their clean and un-
    cluttered look—and their resulting dignity—are of Georgian origin.

18

Classical Revival Architecture

Toward the end of the 1700's the direct influence of ancient Greece and Rome began to be felt in architecture as well as in other arts. Classical forms in colonial and Georgian buildings were derivative, in the sense of having descended from the Italian Renaissance by slow and diluting stages; columned temple fronts for example, independent of the body of the building, were rarely constructed. But with the discovery of the ruins of Pompeii in the mid 1700's, a new, more scientific and archaeological fashion was begun and artists and architects increasingly went directly to the ancient, pre-Christian monuments and ruins for inspiration. In the new United States this appeared first in the classically-derived buildings of Thomas Jefferson 20 (whose own designs, such as his famous home at Monticello, have had a long life in American architecture). Then, about 1820, a national style appeared, the Greek Revival. A passion for the ancient world developed, a passion reflected in education, in the names of new cities and towns (Athens, Utica, Syracuse, and the like), and above all in architecture. The temple front—the columned portico with its triangular pediment above—became a necessary part of all proper architecture; the result, as one foreign visitor remarked, was that you could not tell the function of an American building from the outside, for churches, government buildings, schools, and so on all looked rather alike. But again the building material was almost always wood, and again the ancient originals were by no means always recognizable in the result, for the Greek Revival was not the product of archaeological science or of a need to reproduce ancient buildings exactly. Nor was it all Greek; unfluted, smooth columns 21 appeared, and many other details were often Roman, taken from the books of drawings of ancient monuments, both ruins and restorations, that had become increasingly available.

Northampton, on the tide of fashion, once had a very large, indeed sumptuous, Greek Revival house, the Bowers House (later the Bright House) of 1826. It stood near the corner of Summer and Prospect Streets and was designed by Ithiel Town of New Haven and New York, an architect of rank. It had a full six-columned porch two tall stories high, and the main body of the house, behind the porch, was flanked by extending symmetrical wings, lower but also columned.

20. *Sage Hall, Smith College, at the foot of Green Street, 1924 (Delano and Aldrich); the domed block is adapted from Monticello of the late 1700's*

21

21. *Capen House, Smith College, Prospect Street, 1825* [opposite]
22. *The James House, 42 Gothic Street, 1850; now The People's Institute but
spoken of in a book of 1904 as the 'Household Arts Building of Home Culture Clubs'*
23. *Detail of 22*
24. *Detail of the porch of Dewey House, Smith College campus, 1827*

25. *Duckett House, Smith College, corner of Bedford Terrace and Elm Street*

26. 122 Hawley Street
27. Wright Tomb, Bridge Street Cemetery, 1848

28. *Lodge of the Benevolent and Protective Order of Elks, 43 Center Street*

The Bowers house is gone, but its influence can be seen roundabout, for example in two fine houses side by side on Main Street in neighboring Haydenville. Other grand Greek Revival buildings appeared in Northampton, houses of important citizens. Most used the Ionic order, slender and scrolled, with the details, sometimes archaeologically quite exact, carried out sensitively in wood (ancient architecture is classified according to "orders," or types of columns with their capitals atop and accompanying systems of moldings and proportions).

The effect of the Greek Revival can be seen in numerous buildings that do not have temple fronts—in their porches, pediments, and colonnades. The pediment is everywhere in American architecture as it is in Europe, and until quite recently many architects could hardly design a facade, doorway, or window without it. It is both the logical result of building a rainshedding roof of two sloping surfaces, and of wishing to use the most recognizable architectural symbol of that classical antiquity the founding fathers looked to with such reverence and interest (even our traditional fire boxes take the shape of temple fronts). But, this being America, all kinds of combinations of styles appeared. A dignified five-over-five brick house could be capped by a classical cornice, its lines of moldings and typical accompanying staccato of light and shade binding the surfaces of the building together and giving finish to its edges. The simplicity of design so marvelously expressed in the best ancient Greek architecture caught the imagination of many craftsmen, such as those who designed certain beautiful, austere local tombs. By the time the Civil War broke out the Greek Revival was over, but the sense of historical continuity that temple fronts convey continued to be sought after for a long time, and as a result they are as much a part of the American townscape as the church spire.

28

The Victorian Era

In 1820, when the Greek Revival style began, there were some three thousand people in Northampton; at the end of the nineteenth century there were six times that. The town that so tumultuously welcomed General Lafayette in 1825 had changed greatly by the time Jenny Lind first visited it in 1851. And by 1904, when its two hundred and fiftieth anniversary was celebrated with great fervor, the town had been transformed. A book published to record the events of 1904 has in it a section on historical localities which ends by saying that

> In the last sixty years the center of the town has been almost wholly changed. Hardly a building remains just as it was in 1844. With three or four exceptions, every church edifice, every public building, every store and shop, and every house, on Main Street, have been entirely rebuilt and enlarged, or altered so as to lose their old-time appearance . . . the old landmarks, once so familiar . . . have disappeared.

The tempo of change increased gradually to just after the Civil War and then speeded up enormously: much of what one sees today in downtown Northampton and along certain major streets branching out from the center dates from the years between 1870 and 1900.

These changes in the nature and appearance of the city are suggested by the following facts. In the second half of the 1830's silk cultivation flourished, especially in the Florence area, and with it the planting and care of thousands of mulberry trees. In 1842 the first savings bank opened, and in 1845 the railroad, so important to the growth of the town, arrived from the south (the canal company ceased functioning in 1847). The present City Hall was built in 1850, and in the later 1850's the gas works, the first major river dikes, and the Northampton State Hospital were constructed. Street cars first appeared in 1866, and by 1873 the Northampton Street Railway was in operation, knitting the outlying settlements and Northampton proper together. In 1867 the Clarke School for the Deaf was founded, and in 1875 Smith College opened.

During these forty years the Mill River, whose level drops fairly rapidly along its course southeastwards, powered up to seventy-odd mills. Cutlery, silks, hardware, wood products, and many other arti-

29. *View of the central part of Main Street, south side, about 1910; ten of the thirteen buildings are still standing, though the two furthest to the right have been re-faced*

cles were manufactured both before and after the change-over from waterpower to steam, which took place mostly in the 1870's. By then the terrible war was over and there was a new confidence in the town. The Smith Charities, founded in the late 1840's, put up their offices on Main Street in 1866. In 1872 Memorial Hall was built and, in rapid succession from then to the end of the century, several churches, the County Court House, the railroad station, the Academy of Music, Forbes Library, and many other fine buildings were erected. This is when the most fundamental change in the town took place until the period following World War II. The result was Victorian Northampton, visible in great part today.

32
33

Not so long ago the architecture of this period was thought to be rather unimportant and even ridiculous. But more recently it has become apparent that Victorian buildings record artistic and cultural attitudes as significant in the story of America as those of any other period. These buildings speak of growth, of confidence, and of optimism, of discarding the supposedly confining attitudes of earlier days, of a sense of power and of the need for psychological independence of the intimidating culture of Europe. At first glance, American architecture of the Victorian period seems chaotic, without guiding principles. There seems not to have been any generally accepted idea about how a building—in broad outline—should look, as there had

32. Armory Street, looking northeast [opposite]
33. Turret at the corner of Armory and Pleasant Streets

been, say, in the Georgian or Greek Revival periods. In other words, the Greek Revival was not followed by a single, rival architectural style, clearly defined as to shapes and forms, to which at the time all important buildings were expected to conform. Victorian architecture is quite another thing, exploring many possibilities in design while avoiding those derived from classical sources. Its very variety is its major hallmark, the clear expression of a muscular, youthful society.

The country was looking for itself, as Walt Whitman had said it must. This seeking took many directions, nowhere more than in architecture. What is most important here is probably not so much a lack of artistic unity of forms and shapes as the images that were created—of medieval castles, Parisian palaces, and bold, original designs triumphantly wrought of wood. This will to make images independent of the immediate past was helped along by a need for new kinds of buildings—railroad stations, for example—which had no traditional functions associated with the traditional styles. In other words, art was in a sense freed from a long past, and innovation flourished. This is nowhere more apparent than in Victorian house design, where the architecture of the period is seen in all its moods—exuberant, playful, romantic, or rhetorical; rarely restrained, never timid.

Victorian Houses

Highly individual house designs, such as the extraordinary cylindrical house on Conz Street, had appeared during the Greek Revival period. *34* This almost unique example of a non-rectangular house was built twenty years before the craze for octagonal buildings began in 1848. The chief apostle of octagonal buildings—there is a fine octagon nearby at Amherst College—pointed out that in such a building one can get more usable interior space for a given length of enclosing wall than in a building of traditional rectangular plan. This advantage, dubious perhaps in respect of the room shapes such plans create, is even greater in a house of circular shape. Modern architects have revived the idea.

As the Greek Revival waned, interest in novel expression in wood *35* increased. Armed with books on house design by Andrew Jackson Downing (published from 1841 onward) and inspired by such master architects as Alexander Jackson Davis and Ithiel Town (who were partners), American builders moved rapidly away from classical *36* models. There were technological as well as cultural reasons for this. Wood, the American building material par excellence, had begun to *37* be worked and shaped by machines. The new steam-driven saws helped to simplify and speed up the building process, especially as lumber could so easily and advantageously be cut to a few standard sizes. Together with the invention of the wire nail-making machines, this revolutionized construction, making possible for example the house frame of two-by-fours nailed together, the famous balloon frame (it first appeared in 1833) that soon largely replaced the relatively massive hand-joined and slotted frames of the past. Power-driven lathes and bandsaws encouraged the use of struts, scrolls, *38* brackets, bargeboards (the wavy, perforated, more or less Gothic-looking edgings set along slanting eaves), and a host of original *39* decorative motifs in wood.

Ideologically there was the profound influence of Romanticism, a movement that emphasized emotion at the expense of logical rules. Sir Walter Scott's novels led the way. In America, there was the work of Edgar Allan Poe, which began to appear in the late 1820's. In its simplest terms Romanticism was a reaction to the classical manner, and from 1840 onward its effect on architecture was very strong. *40*

34. *The Strong House, 32 Conz Street, 1829*

35. Detail of the Maltby (formerly Hopkins) House, Smith College, 112 Elm Street, about 1860 (William F. Pratt)
36. The Hill Institute, 83 Pine Street, Florence; 1878

39

110741

38. House at 337 Bridge Street, with bargeboards and Gothic windows

39. Detail of a gable end at 21 Henshaw Avenue
40. Eaves, brackets, and siding at 26 Phillips Place
41. "Cottage" at 45 North Street; about 1848 (perhaps by William F. Pratt, after Downing's Cottage Residences)

45. *Detail of 44*
46. *Gazebo behind 44 Pomeroy Terrace*

47

49. 71 Pomeroy Terrace
50. 219 Elm Street

Houses with elaborate wooden exterior structure and decoration 41
began to appear. "Cottages," as they were called, were much admired 42
—small houses hinting of the medieval past, richly decorated with
brackets holding up spreading eaves and creating powerful plays of 43
light and shade. Bandsaw work became essential to any self-respect- 44
ing house, small or large, and Northampton has splendid examples of 45
this kind of craftsmanship. What these buildings also have in common is a romantic imagery; that is, hints of castles or of cottages deep 46
in the woods, places far away in time and care from the realities of
life. They come in part from the same wellsprings as the battlements
of later apartment houses, armories, and the like. In time the medieval 47, 97
aspect of all this became more pronounced and appeared in the style
known as High Victorian Gothic, which will be discussed in the section on institutional buildings. Masonry versions of the cottages
appeared in due time, the bracketing gone but the rich effects pre- 48
served through the use of bricks of different colors and by bands of
brickwork set in varying patterns, with the bricks frequently set on
the diagonal, creating a stippling or stitching of highlights and
shadows.

At the same time as the bracketed and bargeboarded houses and
cottages were popular, another romantic house type appeared, the

53. *Detail of the house at 55 State Street*

54. Dr. Graham's House, 111 Pleasant Street
55. 289 Elm Street

56. *Detail of Gawith Hall, The Clarke School for the Deaf, Round Hill Road; 1871 (W. R. Ware)*

Italian villa. Based distantly on traditional country houses in Italy, the type was also popularized by the work and writings of Downing and Davis. Its characteristics are a clear blockiness of the major parts, a square tower, and an asymmetrical, irregular relationship between the main block or blocks and the tower. The roofs tend to be flat, and brackets and scrolls may or may not be used. The kind of house that is blocky in shape, is based on a square plan, and is flat-roofed but has no tower, may be a relative or descendant of the Italian villa style. Northampton has splendid examples of these last, in both wood and masonry, sometimes with "Gothic" details in wood and usually with prominent brackets and wide, projecting eaves.

Just after the Civil War the mansard or Second Empire style appeared, named after the double-sloped roof of Paris and the official architecture of the time of Napoleon III (from 1852). It caught on here during the presidency of General Grant, a symbol of affluence, particularly the affluence of mill owners and mercantile barons. Again Northampton has fine examples of the style in both wood and masonry. The double-pitched roofs are immediately apparent, the lower or more vertical slopes of which are pierced by dormers often boldly framed and hooded. There is usually a tower with its own mansard, but the tower, unlike that of the Italian villa, is placed at the center of the building's facade. Window hoods, moldings, and other details show much ingenuity. Sometimes a version appears of one of the pavilions of the New Louvre—the most important Second Empire building in Paris—a simplified, stripped-down version, but with the proportions and roof outline of the original imported intact. Usually Second Empire houses are large, even vast, and tower over any cottages that stand nearby. There are however smaller versions, often very elegantly proportioned. Older houses were sometimes mansarded to keep up with the times, and recently the form has been revived, though with a twist in effect and meaning as will be seen later on.

The boldness of the Italian villa and Second Empire houses comes not only from their rich and complex forms but also from their emphasis upon verticality. In this respect they are in powerful contrast to the five-over-fives of the past. It is interesting that the latter are, comparatively speaking, earth-hugging in their horizontality and perhaps are relatively more expressive of internal security and warmth. The villas and mansards are extroverted. They strongly call attention to themselves, and symbolize the confident, expanding, progressive society whose leaders built them. This quality of extroversion is continued in the last decades of the century in the manner called Queen Anne. Partly of English inspiration, the Queen Anne 58 house has multiple roof surfaces, giving it a complicated silhouette, 59 and a number of different wall planes. Frequently several different materials and textures are used together. There is often a turret, 60 eccentrically placed, but there are no mansards and no "Gothic" details; the detailing, for example in the cornices, tends to be rather classical. A Queen Anne house is usually large and gives an impression of being richly wrought, of promising exciting and irregular in- 61 terior spaces and shapes. Seventy or even eighty windows are not uncommon. Chimneys are emphasized and strongly detailed, and in the last years of the century the turret tended to be absorbed into the 62 body of the building. It took quite a long time for the Queen Anne style to die out, for it was used well into the present century, ever on a smaller scale and with increasingly diluted forms which can be seen by sharp-eyed observers in buildings of no particular style.

One feature of Queen Anne buildings is the frequent use of shingles, and about 1880 a modified Queen Anne manner appeared in which the surface of the building was shingled continuously, even 63 around the contours of curving surfaces such as bays and turrets. By the 1890's completely shingled buildings of various kinds were com- 64 mon, and this handsome and practical vernacular sheathing is still very much in use.

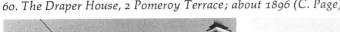

57. *Facades of Chase, Gillett, and Northrop Houses, Smith College, Elm Street;*
Chase House was built about 1810, and the mansard added later [opposite]
58. *The Locke House, 152 South Street; about 1883 (C. S. Jones)*
59. *The Dimock House, Grove Hill, Leeds; 1880 (E. C. Gardiner)*
60. *The Draper House, 2 Pomeroy Terrace; about 1896 (C. Page)*

61. The Hammond House, 222 Elm Street; 1891 (R. F. Putnam)
62. Detail of 61 [opposite]

64. *Detail of shingles at 10 Henshaw Avenue*

Victorian Churches

1   The Edwards Church of 1872 was as Victorian as were contemporary
houses. The spire was covered with multi-colored slates in a bold pattern and the detailing of the walls and eaves was of medieval European inspiration as were the window forms. In a sense the building
could be called eclectic; that is, the result of picking and choosing
among elements from various architectural periods and assembling
them in a building of no recognizably traditional style. This typically
American process can be seen to a greater or lesser degree in almost
all Victorian buildings.

The involvement of post-Civil War church architecture with European medieval architecture was considerable. Again, few if any direct
copies were made, and there is always a feeling in these buildings of
something very American. They would not look right in Europe. This
is partly because of the eclecticism mentioned above and partly because of American craftsmanship and materials. But it is chiefly
because American architects of the period, many if not most of whom
had traveled in Europe and had studied at the Beaux Arts in Paris,
used European buildings only as points of departure or for their details of design. They could admire and appreciate, say, the round-
headed entrances and windows of the Romanesque period, (the
eleventh and twelfth centuries), or the pointed ones of the Gothic
(from the twelfth through the fifteenth centuries), but used them
more for inspiration than for models.

An example of how a talented architect could carry this off is seen
65   in the First Church, the work of the senior partner of a much sought-
after Boston firm. The general outlines are those of a European
church, but closer examination shows a simplified design that evokes,
66   as in the doorways and windows, a certain calm dignity. The historical
detail, in other words, is largely lacking, and the controlling lines of
the design are firm and clean. This can be seen particularly well in the
tower and spire, where a New England economy of detail has replaced
the more agitated silhouettes of Europe. The interior, with its warm
colors and tall iron columns, is one of the best of its kind.

A few years later, on the site of the old Mansion House, St. Mary's
67   Church was built in a modified Gothic manner. The unequal spires

are reminiscent of the famous cathedral of Chartres in France, but the rest of the design is unequivocally Victorian. The fine doorways and the great spreading central window largely dominate the facade, *68* and the modulations of surface front and back are sensitively handled. Again European historical detail is largely lacking, replaced here in part by brick "stitching" and masonry of different textures and colors. It is worthwhile to contrast the design of the taller spire with that of the wooden church of St. Mary, of 1868, in nearby Haydenville, a fine example of provincial wooden "Gothic."

At the end of the century the Episcopal congregation built St. John's Church in a Romanesque manner. As in the case of the other churches, the architect showed considerable freedom of invention and organization. The building looks larger than it is partly because of the bold way the various elements are handled—the big round-headed arches of the facade for example, or the layering of the tower through the use of encircling string cornices at varying heights. The stonework *69* also adds to this feeling of monumentality. The resulting impression is one of near-indestructability, of a solidity nicely judged, not the least because of the excellence of the stonework. *70*

65. *First Church of Christ Congregational, 129 Main Street; 1878 (Peabody & Stearns)*

67. Church of St. Mary of the Assumption, Elm Street; 1881–1885 (P. W. Ford)

69. *St. John's Episcopal Church, tower; 1892–1893 (R. W. Gibson)*
70. *Symbol of St. Matthew, detail of 69*

Institutional Buildings, 1850-1900

These structures reflect many of the modes of design already discussed, but they are in some ways even closer to the currents of contemporary big city architecture in America than the Victorian houses and churches of the town. A turreted tomb can show the influence of romantic medievalism as readily as City Hall, the latter the work of William Fenno Pratt, a local architect. He designed it when he was a young man and he continued to build buildings in the city for nearly forty years. City Hall however does not have a romantic shape, for the body of the building is a plain shoe box-like block; the historical-romantic parts are the turrets and lacework added onto it. The slotted exterior walls and the detailing of the windows are also examples of the inventiveness of the years just before the Civil War, inventiveness not dependent on any classical tradition. Detailing of an equally high order can be seen at the County Jail in the brickwork, the window arches, and the fine old eight-sided cupola. The jail also preserves a pair of granite, doubly-curved exterior staircase skirts of the kind seen soon after on many town buildings. Similar detailing, and a grand example of pre-Civil War institutional planning, can be studied at the State Hospital.

Just after the war Pratt designed the most classical of his buildings, that for The Smith Charities. Of sandstone and thus in step with high Boston fashion, it is composed of an assembly of Italian motifs both ancient and Renaissance, topped with an Italian attic carrying an urn supported on scroll-like forms. The result is dignified and reserved, quite suited to its purpose. The architects of Memorial Hall, on the other hand, who came from the Middle West, produced a building of a modified French character, for the curving roof is as Second Empire as any mansard, and can be seen in the city halls of Boston and Philadelphia of the 1860's and 1870's. In Northampton vertical projecting piers were substituted for the multiplication of columns common in grander examples of this sub-style.

What the architectural historian calls High Victorian Gothic—multicolored, towered, and irregular in outline, with pointed arches and often with a full panoply of crockets and turrets—appears at College Hall, the work of the same man who was to design the First Church a few years later. Bricks of different colors, laid up in various

patterns, appear beside two or three kinds of stone, tooled and fin-
81 ished with various textures that catch the light in different ways.
87 Some of the stone columns were turned on power-driven lathes, a
very Victorian detail. The many arches are banded and striped. And
atop this beautifully sited building is a grand clock tower, its upper-
82 most stage as evocative of a medieval defensive tower as anyone
could want. The same architect also designed the Smith College
83 Alumnae Gymnasium, where the structural brick and stonework and
84 the decorative carving are well worth observing.

Emerging during the heyday of High Victorian Gothic was the manner called Richardsonian Romanesque, after the work of Henry Hobson Richardson (1838–1886), one of the most creative American
85 architects. In Northampton the style is represented by the County
86 Court House and, to a somewhat lesser degree, by the Forbes Library building. Light and dark stone—granite and sandstone in both build-ings—the prominent use of massive, powerful round-headed arches,
87 often resting on short, squat columns, and complex roof systems, are characteristic of this style. As at St. John's Church, a sense of mas-siveness and permanence is conveyed by these buildings, which in their way speak as strongly of a confident America as do the Second Empire and Queen Anne mansions. The Court House tower is very Richardsonian, a simplified version of his Trinity Church tower in Boston of the early 1870's. Northampton was very much up to date.

In the last decade of the nineteenth century the new institutional buildings of the town were designed in a variety of styles. The Academy of Music—the seat of the first municipally supported theater in the United States—is especially interesting as its facade, toward Main Street, is derived from historical, chiefly Italian, sources
88 while its body, as seen from Pulaski Park or along South Street, is very American. That is, it changes character from front to rear ac-cording to the function of the areas enclosed. At the front where the foyer is, the design is quite European, sophisticated and polite. The central body of the building, enclosing the actual auditorium, is less elaborately handled, though it is divided up into bays by brick pilas-ters. But the far or south end of the building, housing the backstage area and the necessary tower-like form or fly (the loft for the scenery gear), is treated like a factory, plain and unadorned except for an abbreviated scallop of brickwork at the eaves line. As the public sig-nificance of the spaces decreases, the architecture, in respect of the use of familiar historical forms, is de-emphasized. Much the same thing appears on Victorian commercial buildings, where elaborate

71. *Tomb, Bridge Street Cemetery; 1849*

TOMB
1849.

72. City Hall, Main Street; 1850 (W. F. Pratt)

76. Detail of 75
77. Stairs at the corner of Main and Center Streets

78. The Smith Charities, 51 Main Street; 1866 (W. F. Pratt)

79. *Memorial Hall, Main Street; 1872–1874 (McLaughlin Brothers)*
80. *Detail of 79*

81. *College Hall, Smith College, west entrance; 1873–1875 (Peabody & Stearns)*
82. *College Hall tower, detail*

83. Alumnae Gymnasium, Smith College; 1890 (Peabody & Stearns)
84. Detail of 83

85. *Hampshire County Court House, Main Street; 1885–1887 (H. F. Kilburn)*
86. *Forbes Library, as seen about 1900 from College Hall Tower; 1893–1895*
(W. C. Brocklesby)
87. *Detail of 85, porch columns and capital*

88. *The Academy of Music, west flank; 1891 (W. C. Brocklesby)*
89. *Facade of 88, detail*
90. *Facade of 88, detail*

91. Lyman Plant House, Smith College, College Lane; from 1892 onward (Lord and Burnham; the gardens were laid out in 1892 by Olmstead and Elliot)

cornices were used only on the front, stopping at the corners.

The facade of the Academy of Music is chiefly of terra cotta, molded and pressed into more or less classical forms. The pilasters, decorated with symbols appropriate to the function of the building, derive from Italian Renaissance architecture of about 1500, whereas the central part of the design, with its scrolls, panels, and advancing and retreating planes and moldings, is in a rather baroque mood; that is, it is related to the chief style of the Catholic countries from about 1600 onward. All in all a most American, and instructive, building.

The following year the Lyman Plant House at Smith College was begun, in its own way as revealing as the Academy of Music. Light-weight structures with wood and metal frames filled in with glass had been made famous and popular by the novel 1851 Crystal Palace in London and its many progeny. At the Lyman Plant House, where one might think there would be little chance for historical reference because of the function of the structure, the builders created a very Victorian building. First, the shapes of the glass roofs are in the French Second Empire manner, as at Memorial Hall. Gothic influence, so strong throughout much of the nineteenth century, appears in the pointed outlines of the entranceway and the windows of the main building. The main roof lines are ridged with metal fleurs-de-lis and finished, like Memorial Hall, with metal versions of the stone crockets atop College Hall tower. Finally, and quite extraordinarily, the garden-side doors are surmounted by a glass fanlight of obviously colonial inspiration. Other late nineteenth century Smith College buildings show this eclecticism, but none so startlingly so. Stoddard Hall leans toward what might be called functional medieval, while at Seelye Hall Italian sixteenth century, Dutch, and English Georgian motifs combine in a sober and quite prepossessing pastiche.

The century was seen out, in architecture, by the battlements and fortified gateway of the Armory. It was the fashion to design armories as fortresses, and there are examples in numerous American cities and towns. Northampton's is one of the best—balanced, colorful, confident. The consistency of its color and the dimensional texture of the brick, applied with hardly any interruption across the face of the building, knit the design together. The entranceway, in direct descent from the fortress gates of the Roman Empire—including the slit windows—strikes a convincing posture of resistance. The other windows are, however, functional in the modern sense; such combinations of historicism and practicality are one of the main features of nineteenth century American institutional architecture.

City cemeteries are almost always rewarding in the study of art and architecture, and the Bridge Street ground is no exception. Apart from the moving and beautiful stones of two and three centuries ago, *9* and tombs that reflect architectural fashions, there is also often a juxtaposition of forms and styles as telling as that on any city street. At Bridge Street obelisks, for millenia symbols of immortality, are *100* sprinkled among the tombstones, and there is an Italianate chamber tomb, as classically proper in its forms as any of the stone mausolea of Europe.

93. Stoddard Hall, Smith College, entrance-way by Elm Street; 1899, and enlarged in 1919.

97. *The Armory, King Street; 1900*
98. *Detail of 97*
99. *Detail of 97*

Nineteenth Century Commercial Buildings

Brick was the chief building material and the patterning of brickwork the chief decoration in Northampton commercial and engineering structures of the last century. In general there are far fewer references in them to the historical past than in other kinds of buildings, *101* though there are exceptions, as in a patterned facade with distinctly *102* Romanesque overtones. Some of the structural stonework of a purely functional kind has the appeal not only of simple strength but also of a quality of texture resulting from the craftsman's sensitive control of his tools. Plain, undecorated architecture has been in high regard for some decades, and the mills of the nineteenth century have gained *103* in appeal. They are honest designs, sometimes of excellent proportions. There is often in good mill architecture a satisfying ratio be- *104* tween solid wall surfaces and windows, and the abstract patterns thus created can be seen as a kind of functional architectural style.

Commercial blocks in the center of town were another matter. For two or three decades after the end of the Civil War it was the fashion *105* to decorate these blocks, especially their assertive cornices, with brickwork patterns. There are many variations in the designs used, but the overall effect is one of homogeneity because of the common denominator of the design unit, the brick. Bricks bring into play the dimensional texture spoken of above, as they are with some excep- *106* tions all the same size. The lively patterns devised by placing the *107* bricks lengthwise and end-on have in common an unavoidable module, or unit of design, the dimensions of the standard brick. The masons who did this work—one feels the cornices are not so much the results of architects' or even of builders' designs on paper as of the inventiveness of the master masons—were artist-craftsmen of a high order. There are dozens of fine patterns in Northampton ranging from rather lacelike to more structural, all of them created from units of fixed size, the humble brick, of about three by four by eight inches.

Unless the building stands on a corner the cornices, whether of the brick-pattern kind or of the traditional and more classical variety, reach only across the street front of the building. The sides of the buildings, if not party or flush to adjacent structures and thus invisible, are universally plain—fine surfaces for painted advertisements. The backs of the commercial blocks are of great interest, as they show how differently the builders and their patrons felt about fronts and rears. The latter are starkly functional, just windows and *108* walls, the workclothes, so to speak, of these buildings, in contrast to the dressed-up appearance of the street fronts. In some cases the backs of downtown commercial buildings can be, to modern eyes, quite handsome, forming abstract patterns of solid and void without any distracting visual accessories.

This is not to suggest that commercial buildings were never consciously grand; quite the contrary. Railroad stations for example were in the early days often of exotic design, and it became all but necessary as the century progressed for cities and towns to have monumental stations, buildings suitably expressive of the fundamental *109* status of the railroads in American life. Richardson was a factor here too, and the Northampton station reflects his influence on the taste of the times: materials of different textures and colors, red slate roofs, fancy dormers, and rather Queen Anne-like chimneys. The sweeping curve of the covered platform, all made of wood, was a sight that could be seen in a hundred towns, as familiar as any in the country until twenty or so years ago.

And downtown city blocks might recall classical motives, especially those built toward the end of the century when part of the architectural profession, led by the great firm of McKim, Mead, and White, turned once again to the architectural style of imperial Rome. One marvelous example of this is a cornice and pediment as richly *110* wrought as any a Roman emperor ever commissioned. Heavy with fruits and flowers, and exhibiting the emblems of its patrons, it is framed by elaborate moldings, brackets, and rosettes in almost exactly the fashion of the third and four centuries A.D.

102. *Arch carrying the railroad over Arch Street, Leeds*

103. Detail of the Vistron Corporation mill on Pine Street, Florence
104. Mill flank, Leeds [opposite]

105. *End of a cornice on Strong Avenue*
106. *Cornice, Main Street*

Waynesburg College Library
Waynesburg, Pa. 15370

108. Backs of the buildings at 102–112 Main Street, from the Armory Street parking lot

109. *The Railroad Station; about 1890*

110. *Detail of the cornice and pediment of the Masonic Building, 25 Main Street;* *1898 (L. D. Bayley)*

Twentieth Century Traditional Buildings.

The story of architecture in our own century revolves around the existence of two fundamentally different concepts: tradition and innovation. Traditional architecture has often been used selectively, as when an institutional building is given increased dignity and authority by the use of classical Roman columns as décor. The 111 Georgian mode has also been used a great deal since 1900 and Northampton has a good example of this revival in the complex of Smith College dormitories known as the Quadrangle. The detailing 112 is authentic, though the buildings themselves tend to be rather free versions of the original Georgian style. The overall effect is that of a 113 miniature Georgian suburb with ample lawns and fine trees. Now and then a vista is created that approximates a view along a Georgian street of long ago. Red brick walls, white-painted wood trim, slate 114 roofs, and a calm and settled dignity produced by symmetry and regular lines are the major features of this Georgian revival architecture, an architecture that still has a following and may yet have a future. It has been used repeatedly in institutional and commercial 115 buildings, sometimes to make a shopping center or a motel appear to be authentically Yankee. It can be successfully reduced to basic una- 116 dorned forms, a process also applied to classical, pillared architecture. 117

Neither bungalows nor stuccoed houses with tile roofs have a particularly remote ancestry, but they belong here because of their tenuous association with traditional ways of building and because they were brought in from outside New England. The word bungalow comes from a Hindustani word meaning "belonging to Bengal," and the building type in America is a one or one-and-a-half story cottage of vaguely Indian origin with a low spreading roof and a deep front 118 porch with pillars. It was a popular kind of small house from about 1910–1930. Partly because it gives less usable space for the size of its floor plan and cellar than other house types it did not flourish here as it did in more temperate parts of the country where cellars are less necessary. Stuccoed houses, originating in Florida and California, never really caught on in New England either, though they do add visual piquancy to our streets when they appear. Some examples 119 carry the stamp of the California mission style, as in the presence of an arcade—in this case of windows in the center section of the second 120

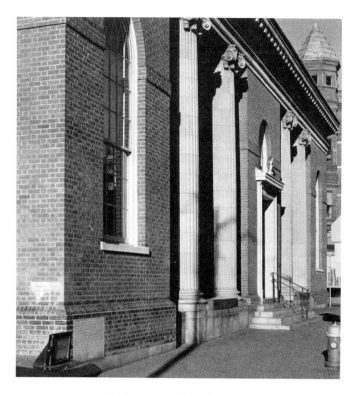

story—a motif that goes back to the arched mission courtyards. The tiles are Mediterranean by way of the Spanish settlers' early structures in this country.

    Other stylistic revivals and survivals flourish as well: Colonial and *121, 153* Cape Cod, for example, and many mixtures of styles and motifs. Northampton's streets, whether in commercial or residential areas, show this compounding of historical periods very suggestively. The visual complexities thus produced are emphasized in turn in the busi- *122* ness areas by the ever-present signs and their extraordinary variety *123* of lettering, colors, shapes, and even by their movement; this is espe- *124* cially true along the strung-out arteries of the city's entrance and exit *125* streets. It is all very American and very familiar, appropriate commercially and a vigorous, representative expression of freedom and *126* feeling as well. On and near these colorful troughs of traffic one finds *127* practical structures of interest and beauty—coal pockets and cement *128, 129* works, for example, and many other remarkable structures. There *130* are sober rows of housing, probably built by paternalistic but responsible mill owners. Finally, if some of the exuberant devices used to *131* call attention to various enterprises were subtracted from our vision *132* the town would be the poorer, and less American.

112. *Air view of the Quadrangle, Smith College, from the east. Bounded by Elm Street, Paradise Road, and Kensington Avenue; 1926–1936 (Ames and Dodge)*
113. *Air view of Comstock and Wilder Houses (upper left-hand corner of 112), seen from the west*

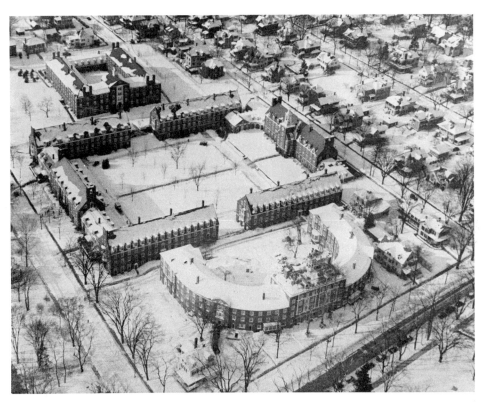

117. 125 Pleasant Street
118. 127 Bridge Street

124. *King Street, looking north*
125. *View northwest from lower Pleasant Street*

126. *Coal pockets at 24 Fulton Avenue, off Pleasant Street*
127. *303 King Street*

128. *Back of 55–65 South Street* [opposite]
129. *2–14 Randolph Place*

132. Haydenville Road, Leeds

Modern Architecture

In Northampton as in many cities and towns modern architecture arrived only after World War II. In the broadest terms the style can be described as the result of rejecting ideas from the historical past and searching for forms, often plain and uncluttered, thought to fit with modern life. In other words the imagery of the past, whether classical or medieval, Italian or English, is denied, and in its place a kind of clear geometry is substituted. This does not mean that decoration, that devices producing patterns of light and shade, have also disappeared, for modern architects achieve such effects from structure, from new materials, and from old materials disposed in new pleasing and eye-catching forms. Sometimes modern architecture is thought of as bare and cold, particularly that phase of it known as the International Style which began in Europe in the 1920's; some however see it as a kind of right-angled poetry in which structure and materials rather than traditional décor form a suitable imagery, one related to machines and their products.

Intimations of non-traditional architecture appeared here as early as the 1920's, as when the blocklike form of a downtown bank build-
133 ing was engraved with what can be described as remnants of classical design (vertical motives reminiscent of fluted columns, for example). But at many points the architect avoided those moldings required in traditional design, as around the windows' edges, and he created decorative details only vaguely historical in pattern. The style—
134 Art Deco or Art Moderne—is just now beginning to be studied; originally it would have caused something of a sensation among those interested in architecture because it departed so sharply from received tradition. Its interior is as important for the time as that of the First Church is for the 1870's; this is true also of the other older downtown bank buildings. What was to come, in the sense of modern attitudes toward the expression of mass and volume, can be seen in the pylons
135 of the Calvin Coolidge Memorial Bridge. They are largely free of
136 historical detail, a kind of engineers' modern architecture quite common in the 1930's, rooted in part in a functional no-nonsense attitude which is one source of modern design.

Here and there one can see examples of what were then radically
137 new building materials, such as structural glass brick. But the town

waited until the 1950's to see modern religious architecture, in the design of the new Edwards Church, with its broad clear lines and 2 somewhat Scandinavian flavor. And it was during the 1950's that 138 Smith College architecture swung from the thoroughly traditional—as in the Helen Hills Hills Chapel, a typical New England Church 139 form—to the crisp lines of Cutter and Ziskind Houses, where there 140 are no decorative details whatsoever from the past. Underneath its 141 historical display the chapel, like the two Houses, has a structural frame of steel.

Since building Cutter and Ziskind the College has preferred modern design. The Clark Science Center hides its supporting structural 142 frame behind sheets of glass and traditional brick and merges well with the lawns and great elms in front of it. The Mendenhall Center for the Performing Arts, composed around a spacious open court, is 143 more highly articulated than the Science Center—that is, it has a greater profusion of parts and therefore of shade and shadow details, and there are a greater number of textures involved. The architecture of Frank Lloyd Wright comes to mind, especially his work in the southwestern desert; another strong influence on the architect was modern Finnish design. The Fine Arts Center, with respect to principles of its design, lies somewhere between the two. Because of its 144 function, which requires among other areas large studio and gallery spaces, it also is more articulated than the Science Center. But that articulation is limited to an unadorned geometry of surfaces: half-cylinders, sloping prisms, and simple rectangles. It is partly clothed in square terra cotta tiles that to a degree tie it visually to its venerable neighbor, College Hall.

Local government, in its recent building ventures, has also clearly gone modern, for example in the Court House additions and the Housing for the Elderly. The succession of County court buildings in a line along Gothic Street says a lot about architectural history in our country: first Richardsonian Romanesque, the High Style of the 1880's; then Neo-Georgian—polite, acceptable, harmonious with its surroundings and with American traditions; and now cement blocks 145 and smoky glass in a frank and uncluttered geometry. At the Housing for the Elderly, pre-manufactured structural units of reinforced con- 146 crete have been assembled to produce one of the largest buildings in the city, a well-proportioned design that does not strive for garish effects and that should wear well visually.

Business interests, sometimes requiring economical, functional construction, sometimes in the quest of current fashion, have built 147

133. Corner of Main and King Streets, Main Street side, detail; 1928
(J. W. Beal Sons)
134. Upper east corner of the same building

135. Calvin Coolidge Memorial Bridge, detail of pylon; 1939
136. Calvin Coolidge Memorial Bridge; 1939

137. 240 Bridge Street

138. *View from inside the Edwards Congregational Church, 297 Main Street, to the D. A. Sullivan School; 1958 (H. E. Wagoner)*

*140. Air view of Cutter and Ziskind Houses, Smith College, Elm Street; 1957
(Skidmore, Owings, & Merrill)
141. Southeast flank of Cutter House*

142. *McConnell Hall of the Clark Science Center, Smith College campus; 1965 (Shepley, Bulfinch, Richardson, & Abbott)*
143. *The Mendenhall Center for the Performing Arts, Smith College, Green Street, courtyard and theater building; 1968 (Westermann, Miller, & Associates)*

144. *Hillyer Hall of the Fine Arts Center, Smith College, Elm Street; 1972*
(J. Andrews)

145. Additions to the County Court House facilities along Gothic Street. Nearest, newest portion, 1974 (Drummey Rosane Anderson); middle part, 1928 (K. S. Putnam)

146. *Housing for the Elderly, Conz Street; 1975 (Reinhardt and Associates)*

147. Store entrance, shopping plaza off North King Street

148. Parking lot, shopping plaza off North King Street

the widest variety of designs in recent times. Many are standardized, to a very considerable degree, all over the country. Inevitably many are surrounded by acres of parking lots which, when empty, have
148 something of the quality of a lunar landscape. Right now the rage is for a curious kind of mansard, the slanting feature, half wall and half
149 roof and often shingled, that appears over and over on restaurants,
150 hotels and motels, shops, apartment buildings, service stations, and
151 business offices. Sometimes it is more of an eave and roof and some-
152 times it emerges as a sloping portion of wall, creating a rather Egyptian look. Possibly it is a revival of one of the main features of the Second Empire style that flourished after the Civil War, or perhaps it is related to the massive, sloping forms of the Mayan ruins in Central America, a kind of Mansard Mayan, a twentieth century answer to such nineteenth century marvels as Lumberyard Baroque and Carpenter's Frenzy.

In modern housing since World War II the major tendency has been to build one or another form of the ranch house, much-modified descendants of Frank Lloyd Wright's spectacularly original Prairie Houses of the turn of this century. And some have preferred the old
153 ways, building houses modern in structure and fittings but retaining the look of the confidence and security of the past, symbols of the more permanent aspects of our experience. As the city has grown,
154 especially toward the north and west, new houses have been built by the score where there were broad meadows and pastures only a few years ago.

*   *   *   *   *

THIS is not to say that no atmosphere of countryside exists. Quite the contrary: there are farmlands, the banks of the Connecticut are
155 still nature's own out of respect for the river's power, and there are
156 many pockets and parcels of land free of all buildings. But inevitably the face of the land has changed a good deal, particularly along north-south lines. First there was the old coach track. Then the railroad
157 came, roughly parallel to it. By widening and paving the coach road, what is now Route 5 was created, for decades the main thoroughfare connecting the town with its neighbors up and down the river. In the
158 late 1960's the double expressways of Interstate 91 arrived, cutting across the Ox Bow in a great sweeping curve as they too follow the ancient valley route of river, coach road, and railroad. In an extension of urban tentacles ever further from the center of the city, structures

have been built along this route to serve both local traffic and long-distance travelers.

But in and near the city proper are many quite unspoiled natural *159* features such as Paradise Pond, formed by a dam in the Mill River *160* and the steep natural contours behind it. There are fine parks, the *161* gifts of town residents, and numerous private gardens and the well- *162* kept grounds of private and public institutions. The Smith College *163* campus is sprinkled with rare plants, shrubs, and trees. Above all, with respect to natural features, one appreciates the town's trees—for their own sake as things of beauty and for their partnership with buildings as well. They soften the harsh affects of some designs and enhance the good qualities of others. Without trees, without their *86* rippled contours and their shade, standing around a building or *164* marking the progress of a street, town architecture would be a very *165* different matter and diminished. Even in winter they enrich our *166* vision. Something of this is revealed when, sadly, great elms come down and buildings nearby become unfamiliarly bare, or a street is robbed of some of its comforting natural dignity. Fortunately, most of the trees in Northampton—oaks, beeches, maples, birches, poplars, chestnuts, pines, hemlocks, and others—seem prosperous and their species permanent.

149. 167 South Street
150. Detail of hotel at I-91 Interchange

151. 344 King Street
152. Entranceway at an apartment complex at 80 Damon Road

153. 179 Elm Street; 1953
154. Air view of Ryan Road, looking northeast, with Acrebrook Drive at the lower right-hand corner

156. *Fitzgerald Lake, seen from Rick Drive*

157. *Air view of the railroad and Route 5 between the River and the Ox Bow south of the city, looking north*

*162. The Summer House in Child's Park, between North Elm and Prospect Streets;
K. S. Putnam*
163. Smith College rose garden at 10 Prospect Street

166. *Air view of part of the city's center, looking northeast*

Reading List

A. Historical and Cultural Background

J. G. HOLLAND, *History of Western Massachusetts. The Counties of Hampden, Hampshire, Franklin, and Berkshire* (Springfield, Mass. 1855)

J. R. GILFILLAN, *Northampton in the Spanish American War* (Easthampton 1899)

C. JOHNSON, *Historic Hampshire in the Connecticut Valley* (Springfield, Mass. 1932)

V. W. BROOKS, *The Flowering of New England* (New York 1936), and *New England: Indian Summer* (New York 1940)

River Gods. Their Story in the Pioneer Valley, Massachusetts (Northampton 1941)

The Hampshire History, Celebrating 300 Years of Hampshire County, Massachusetts (Northampton 1964)

E. S. GAUSTAD, *The Great Awakening in New England* (Chicago 1968)

B. Primary Sources, Biography, and Genealogy

Judd Manuscripts, in the Forbes Library, Northampton (on microfilm, covering the period 1650–1833)

S. CLARK, *Antiquities, Historicals, and Graduates* (Northampton 1882)

Centennial Hampshire Gazette, 6 September 1886

Early Northampton (Betty Allen Chapter, D. A. R., Northampton 1914)

C. F. WARNER, *Representative Families of Northampton* (Northampton 1917)

L. E. DE FOREST, ed., *The Journals and Papers of Seth Pomeroy, Sometime General in the Colonial Service* (New Haven 1926)

WORKS PROGRESS ADMINISTRATION, *Index to the Daily Hampshire Gazette 1786–1937* (1939)

R. B. NYE, *George Bancroft, Brahmin Rebel* (New York 1944)

P. MILLER, *Jonathan Edwards* (New York 1949)

E. C. LATHEM, ed., *Meet Calvin Coolidge, the Man Behind the Myth* (Brattleboro 1960)

O. E. WINSLOW, *Jonathan Edwards, 1703–1758* (New York 1961)

C. City Histories and Memorial Volumes

J. PAUL, *The Mill River Disaster* (Springfield, Mass. 1874)

Picturesque Hampshire. A Supplement to the Quarter-Centennial Journal (Northampton, Nov. 1890)

F. N. KNEELAND, *Northampton, The Meadow City* (Northampton 1894)

C. A. SHEFFELD, *A History of Florence* (Springfield, Mass. 1894)

J. R. TRUMBULL, *History of Northampton, Massachusetts, from its Settlement in 1654*, 2 vols. (Northampton 1898–1902)

H. S. GERE, *Reminiscences of Old Northampton, 1840–1850* (Northampton 1902)

F. KNAB, *Northampton of Today, Depicted by Pen and Camera* (Northampton 1902)

The Meadow City's Quarter-Millennial Book (Northampton 1904)

A. H. CARPENTER, *Northampton, Past and Present* (Springfield, Mass. 1911)

A. HANNAY, *A Chronicle of Industry on the Mill River* (Northampton 1936)

Northampton and the Northampton Institution for Savings (Northampton 1942)

B. GILMORE, *A Puritan Town and its Imprints, Northampton 1786–1845* (Northampton 1942)

THE TERCENTENARY COMMITTEE, *The Northampton Book* (Northampton 1954)

G. CESTRE, *Northampton Massachusetts. Évolution urbaine* (Paris 1963)

D. Maps, Surveys, Gazetteers, and Directories

J. DENISON, *Map of Northampton Drawn October and November 1794*

MASSACHUSETTS GENERAL COURT, *Map of Northampton* (Boston 1830)

J. G. HALES, *Plan of the Town of Northampton in the County of Hampshire* (Boston 1831)

F. W. BEERS, *The County Atlas of Hampshire, Massachusetts* (New York 1873)

Historical Register and General Directory of Northampton (Northampton 1875–1876)

W. B. GAY, *Gazetteer of Hampshire County, Massachusetts* (Syracuse 1886)

D. L. MILLER, *Atlas of the City of Northampton and Town of Easthampton* (Philadelphia 1895)

Northampton-Easthampton City Directory (New Haven 1974; published annually)

E. Architectural History

H. MORRISON, *Early American Architecture From the First Colonial Settlements to the National Period* (New York 1952)

T. HAMLIN, *Architecture Through the Ages*, revised ed. (New York 1953)

W. ANDREWS, *Architecture, Ambition, and Americans* (New York 1955)

J. E. BURCHARD and A. BUSH-BROWN, *The Architecture of America—A Social and Cultural History* (Boston 1961)

H. A. MILLON and A. FRAZER, *Key Monuments of the History of Architecture* (New York 1965)

H.-R. HITCHCOCK, *Architecture: Nineteenth and Twentieth Centuries* (Harmondsworth 1969)

W. H. PIERSON, Jr., and W. H. JORDY, *American Buildings and their Architects*, 4 vols. (New York 1970–1972)

G. CLAY, *Close-Up: How to Read the American City* (New York 1973)

F. Architectural Styles and Building Types

H. R. SHURTLEFF, *The Log Cabin Myth* (Cambridge, Mass. 1939)

V. J. SCULLY, Jr., "Romantic Rationalism and the Expression of Structure in Wood: Downing . . . and the 'Stick Style,' 1840–1876," in the *Art Bulletin*, vol. 35 (1953), pp. 121–142, and *The Shingle Style. Architectural Theory and Design from Richardson to the Origins of Wright* (New Haven 1955)

C. L. V. MEEKS, *The Railroad Station. An Architectural History* (New Haven 1956)

J. MAASS, *The Gingerbread Age. A View of Victorian America* (New York 1957)

E. A. CONNALLY, "The Cape Cod House: An Introductory Study," in the *Journal of the Society of Architectural Historians*, vol. 19 (1960), pp. 47–56

T. HAMLIN, *Greek Revival Architecture in America* (New York 1964, a reprint of the original ed. of 1944)

J. SUMMERSON, *The Classical Language of Architecture* (London 1964)

H.-R. HITCHCOCK and P. JOHNSON, *The International Style*, revised ed. (New York 1966)

N. PEVSNER, *The Sources of Modern Architecture and Design* (London 1968)

M. WHIFFEN, *American Architecture Since 1780. A Guide to the Styles* (Cambridge, Mass. 1969)

J. BARNARD, *The Decorative Tradition* (London 1973)

G. Northampton Architecture and Buildings

K. S. PUTNAM, *Some Comments on Buildings in the Course of a Walk from Bridge Street to Round Hill*, an undated pamphlet
Some Old Northampton Houses (Northampton 1909)
K. S. PUTNAM, "Northampton Architecture: A Sequence," in *The Northampton Book* (Northampton 1954), pp. 141–160

H. Builders' Handbooks

B. LANGLEY, *The Builder's Jewel, Or, the Youth's Instructor, and Workman's Remembrancer . . . for Drawing and Working, I: The Five Orders of Columns Entire . . . , &c. &c.* (Boston 1800, but originally published in London in 1741)
O. BIDDLE, *The Young Carpenter's Assistant, or A System of Architecture, Adapted to the Style of Building in the United States* (Philadelphia 1805); all of these American handbooks went through many subsequent editions and revisions after the dates given in this list
A. BENJAMIN, *The American Builder's Companion* (Boston 1806)
I. TOWN, *A Description of Ithiel Town's Improvements in the Construction of Wood and Iron Bridges . . .* (New Haven 1821)
A. J. DAVIS, *Rural Residences, etc., Consisting of Designs, Original and Selected, for Cottages, Farmhouses, Villas . . .* (New York 1837)
A. J. DOWNING, *Cottage Residences; or, A Series of Designs . . .* (New York 1842), and *The Architecture of Country Houses* (New York 1850)
W. BROWN, *The Carpenter's Assistant; Containing a Succinct Account of Egyptian, Grecian, and Roman Architecture . . .* (Worcester, Boston, & New York 1848)
S. SLOAN, *American Houses . . .* (Philadelphia 1861)
Palliser's American Architecture, Or Everyman a Complete Builder (New York 1888), and many other Palliser titles in the 1880's and 1890's
The Radford American Homes. 100 House Plans, Price $1.00 (Riverside, Ill. 1903)
H.-R. HITCHCOCK, *American Architectural Books. A List of Books, Portfolios, and Pamphlets on Architecture and Related Subjects Published in America Before 1895*, new printing (Minneapolis 1962)

I. Building Arts and Crafts

M. S. BRIGGS. *A Short History of the Building Crafts* (Oxford 1925)
A. P. MILLS, H. W. HAYWARD, and L. F. RADER, *Materials of Construction*, 5th ed. (New York 1939)
S. GIEDION, *Space, Time, and Architecture*, 3rd ed. (Cambridge, Mass. 1954), Part V, pp. 333–424
E. SLOANE. *American Barns and Covered Bridges* (New York 1954), and *A Reverence for Wood* (New York 1965)
A. K. FINCH, *The Story of Engineering* (Garden City, N.Y. 1960)
N. DAVEY, *A History of Building Materials* (London 1961)
C. W. CONDIT, *American Building. Materials and Techniques from the Beginning of the Colonial Settlements to the Present* (Chicago 1968)
R. JENSEN, "Board and Batten Siding and the Balloon Frame . . . ," in the *Journal of the Society of Architectural Historians*, vol. 30 (1971), pp. 40–50

J. Architects

[For Davis, Downing, and Town, see also Section H, above; for W. F. Pratt see the *Index to the Gazette* listed under Section B, above]

R. H. NEWTON, *Town and Davis, Architects . . .* (New York 1942)

H.-R. HITCHCOCK, *The Architecture of H. H. Richardson and His Times*, revised ed. (Hamden, Conn. 1961)

E. KAUFMANN and B. RAEBURN, *Frank Lloyd Wright. Writings and Buildings* (New York 1960)

H.-R. HITCHCOCK and E. DANZ, *Architecture of Skidmore, Owings & Merrill, 1950–1962* (New York 1963)

D. GUINESS and J. T. SADLER, Jr., *Mr. Jefferson Architect* (New York 1973)

W. A. HOLDEN, "The Peabody Touch: Peabody and Stearns of Boston, 1870–1917," in the *Journal of the Society of Architectural Historians*, vol. 32 (1973), pp. 114–131

Office door, second floor, at 25 Main Street

Index

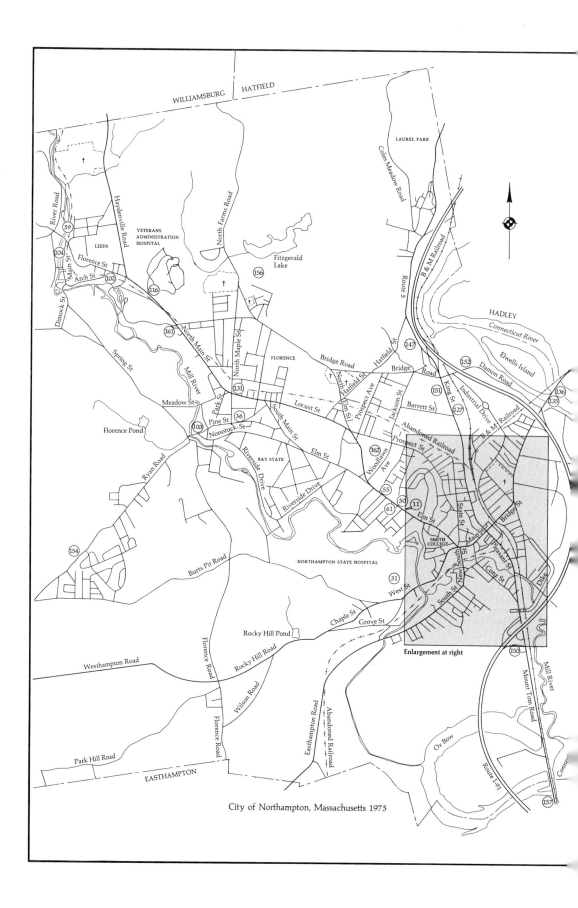

City of Northampton, Massachusetts 1975

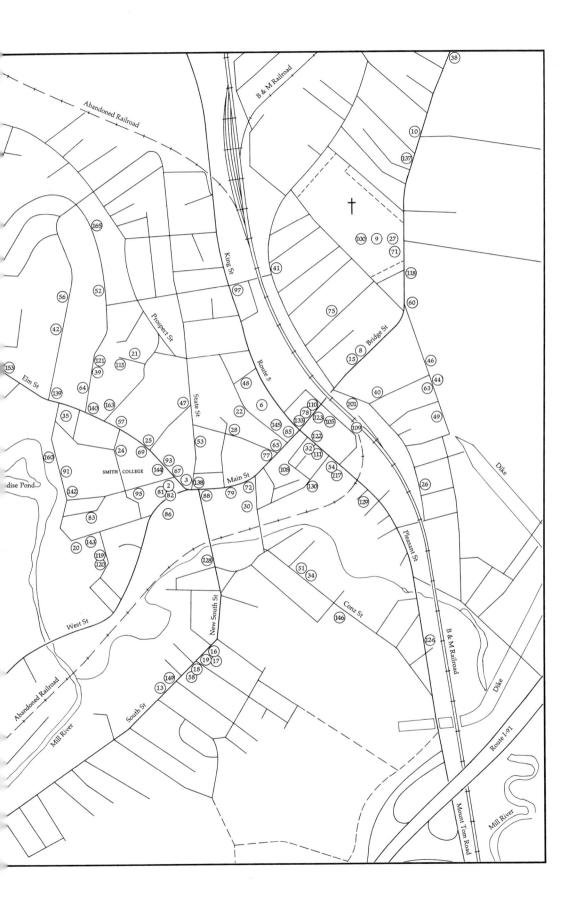

Waynesburg College Library
Waynesburg, Pa. 15370

Waynesburg College Library
Waynesburg, Pa. 15370